STORIES OF A TUMBLEWEED

STORIES
OF A
TUMBLEWEED

Poems

from the desert to the heart

Written and illustrated by
ANDREA BALINT

STORIES OF A TUMBLEWEED
Copyright © 2010 by Andrea Balint

Poems, illustrations, cover design: Andrea Balint
Photo of the author: Ivan Karpati
Photo of the polluted desert: Lench Archuleta

ISBN: 978-0-9789627-0-8
Library of Congress Control Number: 2010939716

All rights reserved. No part of this publication may be reproduced by any mechanical, photographic, or electronic process, or in the form of phonographic recording; nor may it be stored in a retrieval system, transmitted, or otherwise be copied for public or private use without prior written permission.

Send permission requests to:

Permissions
Business Coach Press
1885 Castle Oaks Court
Walnut Creek, CA 94595

or email: info@businesscoachpress.com

Printed in the United States of America
9 8 7 6 5 4 3 2 1

To my Mom and Dad, who gave me the World,

and

to Lench, who taught me to see the magic in it.

ACKNOWLEDGMENTS

First, my unending gratitude to God and to the Spirit world for all their inspiration and for holding my hand in the world of unknown.

To my dear friend, Lucy Munoz, whose invitation to Lench Archuleta's workshop in London led to my life-changing journey and to the birth of this book. My thanks also to my "Earth Angel" friends - Krisztina Felkai, Annamaria Hazay, Anita Horvath, Tamara Menyhart, Agnes Csizmas, Dave van Eif, Sonia Duran, Ayk Oral, Som Dasgupta, Lei Zhang and Damien McDowell - for their love and faith in me, for sharing my enthusiasm and for their wonderful friendship.

I also would like to thank Steven Hilferty and Sandy Patel, who always give me practical advice and ground me when I fly too close to the Sun; and who provided enormous help in publishing this book.

I will always be grateful to my family for their endless love, understanding and patience during my journey in the desert and while I was writing this book; and for fully accepting me the way I am.

I also would like to thank the Archuleta family and Bill and Melinda Hutton for their love, acceptance and their tremendous support during my stay in Arizona and beyond. You will always be in my heart.

Many thanks to James Stewart, my "first reader", who made sure that my spelling and grammatical mistakes were corrected. Your help was invaluable to me.

And finally, I give my thanks and gratitude to all those who have given me their stories and shared their journey with me, from a couple of steps and seconds to many miles and years. I would not be who I am now without you.

TABLE OF CONTENTS

FOREWORD 1

STORIES OF MY JOURNEY 5
    Thousand faces..7
    The beginning..9
    The sacred riverbed 12
    The key to the unknown 14
    The journey of a dream 16
    The transformation 19
    Ceremony 21
    Warriors of love 22
    Almost goodbye..24
    Making a U-turn 26
    Lost 30
    Return to innocence 33
    A moment of truth..34

STORIES OF LIFE 35
    Touch 37

The dance 39

The story of a tumbleweed 43

The garden 45

The door of now 46

The masquerade 47

Running into the deep forest 49

Shadow and light 51

The story of a tree 53

Subtleties 58

Flow 60

Silence 61

Tomorrow 62

Reflection 63

STORIES OF LOVE 65

Something ended 67

A tale of love 69

Goodbye 74

The bird of freedom 75

When eyes meet 78

The gift 79

No words 81

Because of you	82
A late smile	83
The miracle of love	84
Heart	85
Waves of the ocean	86
You and I	88
Tell me everything	90
Mirrors	91
Long distance relationship	92
Missing you	93
Our journey	94

FOREWORD

In the Native American tradition, the tumbleweed is the storyteller. It rolls from place to place, gathers stories and shares them with everyone it meets during its journey. This book contains my tumbleweed stories. Stories that were inspired by the desert and by my journey. Stories that come from my heart to inspire your heart and your journey.

I was born in Hungary, a small country in Europe. Since I was small, I was fascinated by the world, by its wonders, natural and manmade, and by the diversity of people and cultures. Growing up, the real dessert on our Sunday family lunches was that my Dad used to bring the World Atlas to our dining table. We opened it at random and mind-traveled to exciting distant places and gathered memories and adventures of our imagination.

As an adult I was fortunate to get a job abroad, and I lived more than eight years in several countries. During this time I grabbed every occasion to meet people from those distant places and to explore their homelands. I met many wonderful people from all around the world, who shared their friendship, their culture, their knowledge and their stories with me. I traveled to almost all countries in Europe and ventured to some far places in America, Asia and Africa.

The tumbleweed that was born at the dining table of my family grew up during my time abroad and my travels. But I was still walking because I did not know how to roll.

In 2008, while living in London, UK, I attended a workshop led by a Native American shaman and wise man, Lench Archuleta. He left the Sonoran desert in Arizona and crossed the ocean to spread an ancient wisdom, which is by now pretty much forgotten. Things like the importance of giving first before you take; honoring everything and everyone around you; and living in harmony with and respecting nature. His presence and words were so powerful that right then I decided that one day I would visit him to learn more.

That 'one day' happened in May 2010. After more than two days of continuous travel from Hungary, I stepped into the world of the Sonoran desert. Originally I came to Arizona to spend two weeks in the desert, but when the time arrived to return home I was not yet ready. I took a bold step and returned to the desert from the airport for another one and the half months instead of going home. When I left the desert this time, I was not the same. I was not walking any more. I was rolling. And I received this book as a gift.

The stories in this book are told in the form of short poems. The poems are like wrapping paper around a gift. But they wrap instead a thought or a feeling that I would like to share with you, that I want you to open, taste, experience or think about. Once you taste these poems, they will take you to those places I visited and they will give you your own stories.

I wish you a good journey.

With love,

Andrea "Tumbleweed" Balint

STORIES
OF
MY JOURNEY

Thousand faces

When I go to the desert
I always have a fresh eye,
I never know
what I am going to find.

Sometimes treasures
to take them home,
sometimes the wisdom
of an elder or the wind

Sometimes love
of a grandmother tree,
sometimes pain
from a careless touch.

Some places are gentle,
some places are rough.
Some places are light,
some spread shadow.

Some places make me sing,

some make me cry.

All places are unique and different,

none of them are the same.

The desert has a thousand faces, like man.

When I meet people

I always have a fresh eye,

I never know

what I am going to find.

The beginning

I want to be free.
Free like the bird
that flies across the skies,
without worries we have
about life, food, opinion of others.

But I need to fight my fears first,
the strongest that hides the truth,
that makes me lie
to defend or look good.

I didn't understand its power
until yesterday.
But now I feel something changing.

When I hide the truth
I feel pain,
stronger than before,
even in my dreams.

A pain of shame
of not being myself,
of not being responsible
for my actions or my thoughts.

There is a much bigger power
whom I want to look good to,
not the people.

It's my own soul.

No more lies,
no more compromise!

I took my first step
on the path of truth,
abandoned the old path
for the only one that's right for me.

It looks rough, with monsters of the past
that will try to pull me off,
but they have no longer power over me.

I just keep walking,

nod my head to greet them,

then I pass them.

I stay on this path,

my heart will guide me,

and one day…

I will fly.

The sacred riverbed

I walk in the riverbed
searching for stones,
stones of fears that hold me back.
I am on a sacred journey.
I am in a sacred place.

But I step on empty gunshells,
nails in trashed planks hurt my knee
when I kneel down to pick my stone.
Car tires block my way,
the wind carries the sound of gun-shooting
instead of the songs of birds.

I am deeply saddened.
Can't help, but get angry,
angry at those who do not understand,
or at least respect those
who honor this place.

I wish it could be different.
I wish Mother Earth would defend herself
right at the spot
to teach them a lesson.

But she holds her power back
with a teardrop on her face,
and still loves us in her gentle way.
I understand and feel her pain
and of those who love this land.

I wish we all changed today
so that this ravage quickly ends,
so that the river can freely flow
in a sacred riverbed
and the dove's song could fill the wind again.

The key to the unknown

My life at home
was like a battlefield,
constant struggle
with people and work,
constant noise in my head,
constant pain in my gut.

I came to the desert seeking for peace,
peace with myself and the entire world.

I got to learn here
I had the key all the time,
but I was unaware,
unaware of its existence in me.

Now I am learning to use it
to unlock the powers
that were locked down in me
for many many years,
locked down by my fears and beliefs.

I do not know what I am going to find

when I unlock them all.

I do not know

what the world will then look like.

But I feel excited

to use the key over and over again.

I feel the power

slowly coming back to me.

I feel everything is possible.

I see my world changing for the better.

And this is just the beginning....

The journey of a dream

I have a dream.
I go for it.
I want to make it happen.
I get it.
And when I hold it in my hands,
I am not happy.

So I run for another dream,
hoping that will be different.
But I fail again.

What is wrong?
What is wrong with me?
I did my best to get there.

I have forgotten something.
All I wanted was to get:
what I wanted,
the way I wanted.

I missed the miracles on my way,

that were given to me as a gift.

I was so in control of my way

that I missed to enjoy

the sidewalks of my path,

or just sit a little

for the beauty of being there.

I have missed my journey...

What I have left

are the glimpses of moments

that made me happy

not the dream itself.

I have learnt the lesson:
The journey makes you happy
not the destination.

All the little moments are special
when lived through
being aware.

The dream is the future,
the journey is the now.
I need to be present
not to miss my journey again.

There is much more at stake now
than a dream:

IT IS MY LIFE.

It is time to miss no more,
and it is time to live again.

The transformation

I am sitting on a giant rock
at a peaceful spot in the desert.
I am facing the mountain
surrounded by cacti and bushes.

Little lizards come
sunbathing next to me.
The sun touches my face.
The wind blows and
brings some breeze.
Hawks are circling on the sky.
And I am singing a song.

I am at a sacred place,
at the feet of the vastness of nature.

Nothing is as it seems.

I am in a temple
at the altar of the most sacred isle
facing God himself.

I am surrounded by spirits
who came to guide and comfort me
and to witness my transformation.

I feel their loving presence.
I take my time
to honor them and the moment.
I breathe them in.

And in the next moment
a warrior's song
is carried by the wind…

Ceremony

Cold dew baptizes me at dawn

Earth marks my skin

Residue of fire of the sacred sage prepares my soul

Eastern wind strokes my face

My entire being is prepared for this moment

One chance to honor God and my soul

No words can express how it felt to sing and dance on the podium of nature

Years from now I will still remember….

Warriors of love

Today we celebrate
the birth of two warriors.
Our new self has been born
on the ashes of the old,
by spirit completely transformed.

Our birth was witnessed
by nature and by God.
They heard us singing on our rock
mourning the past, welcoming the new
committing to walk on the path of love.

We sang, danced, celebrated,
we were alive in the moment.
We embraced the past
with tenderness and care,
we gave new stories to the wind to carry away.

After our yell, when we left our rocks,

we were free, complete and one with all.

. This moment will never leave us

and we keep walking

hand in hand, alone.

To Damian, my warrior brother

Almost goodbye

Yesterday

I was listening

to the bees under the mesquite tree.

Yesterday

I asked the chaparral for seeds

to take them home.

Yesterday

my feet were free

and dirty.

Yesterday

I was in the desert.

On my last day

I cherish every moment

this day can bring to me.

I breathe in

the wind,

the desert,

and the people

I take them all

with me

until we meet again…

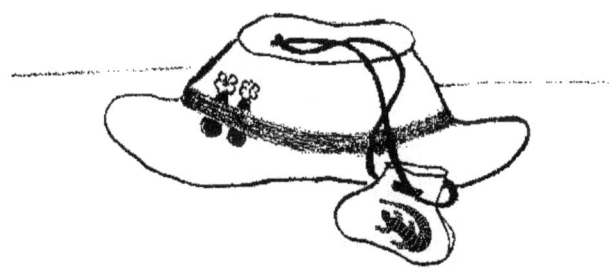

Making a U-turn

Why do I feel this way?
I do not know.

Why do I go back?
I do not know.

Would there be another chance
if I do not go back now?
I do not know.

What will I learn?
I do not know.

Can I afford it?
I do not know.

Is it an escape or a direction?
I do not know.

When will I leave?

My ticket has a date printed on,

but I do not know.

But I know

I have no peace in my heart,

I do not fit in my world.

Mixed up with feelings and responsibility

I am balancing on a fine line

but constantly falling off.

I do not want to fight

but end up in war

with myself and

with everyone around.

I am aware when I go wrong

but still dancing around that fine line

losing my balance

instead of walking straight.

How to live in this world

full of unconsciousness

with the wisdom I learnt?

I want to know.

How to live in truth

in a world full of lies?

I want to know.

How to connect

with the wind, the birds,

the ancients and the Earth?

I want to know.

How to survive the sadness

caused by unconsciousness in the heart?

I want to know.

What direction to take

when I leave the desert next time?

I want to know.

What is the extent of the power

of my heart?

I want to know.

I want to feel.

I want to experience.

I was reborn in the desert

but left too soon.

I ran away too fast.

I am coming back now

to learn to walk.

Lost

I am back to a place
I honor dearly,
I am back to a place
yet to be discovered.
I am back to the desert,
I am back in the West.

I was frozen in the North,
did not know how to keep warm.
I could not hear
my voice in the noise
and when I heard it
I was paralyzed.

It is such a wonderful night
I decide to sleep under the skies
that I never did before.
In the quiet night
by the serenade of crickets
the numbness starts to release.

I can hear my voice now,

calm and reassuring

but I still can't trust myself.

I realize, I can't even trust God.

I lay in complete darkness

just tiny stars dim the skies.

Suddenly the moon comes up,

covering me and everything around with light.

I can see now

but I still can't fall asleep,

I still can't surrender myself to the dream.

I am exhausted,

but still holding up.

I decide not to return to the house.

It would be easier now to get to bed

but I want to learn

to trust and surrender.

I welcome the dawn,

I hear the birds' first song

of the new day.

Sleepless the entire night

now I start to understand

why I got lost…

Return to innocence

I don't know what I am looking for
But I feel alive
Today
I laughed
s
a
I danced   I
g
c   I   created
o   n
n   p   j
t   l   o
e   a   y
magic was on my way I helped
p   e   d
I learned wisdom   d
a
t
I felt and cried
d
        l
        o
        v
        e
        I died
        o
        p
        myself up to
          n   h
          e   e
          d
                  u
                  n
                  k
                  n
                  o
                  w
                  n.

A moment of truth

I've spent most of my life
searching for my path
trying to find out
what my life purpose was,
trying to find enlightenment
to see only what's good.

And just realizing…

There is no such thing
as life without pain.
There is no such thing
as a life purpose.
There is just one thing
called LIFE.

And I've been walking my path all along…

STORIES OF LIFE

Touch

Every second
invisible arms are wrapped around us:
the sunlight, the air, the earth,
even our shadow.

We are touched
by all that surrounds.

Touch is magic,
can take any shape
a smile, a good word,
a caressing hand.

Even life begins with a touch

and ends with a touch

to close our eyes.

Some touch lasts for a second,

some for a lifetime

or even multiple lives

to connect souls.

Touch is a gift

of every moment,

a gift to be shared

with as many as we can.

There is no life

without touch.

Touch all

to live life again.

The dance

I am blind(folded).

I can't see.

I listen to the music

and slowly step outside.

I anchor my directions

to what I hear and know.

I start walking.

I can't find my balance,

I can't see where I am going

but I feel the music

unlocking the rhythm in me.

I can't walk any longer.

I start to dance.

I am seeking harmony with the music.

My steps are uneven

and sometimes I fall

but I stand up

and start dancing again.

The music moves me.

Every second a new step unfolds.

Every move feels different.

I touch different grounds.

I enjoy the dance.

With every move

I am more balanced.

I realize balance

has nothing to do with what I see.

Now I feel the dance.

I spin around and jump.

I try out new moves

but I get dizzy

and I have to stop

as I lose my sense of direction.

I stand still and listen.

I search for my anchors

and move back to them.

I could decide to stay close

and hold onto them.

But I start walking away

To discover new places

where I can dance.

And I start dancing again,

even better than before.

Then I venture to a part of my space

where I step on a sharp rock.

I feel the most intense pain.

I fall down

with teardrops on my face.

I reflect on what I feel

and as I learn this place

the pain dissolves.

I sit there

not wanting yet to move.

But I feel the music

spreading in my veins,

my body follows

and I stand up

and start dancing again:

the dance of life.....

The story of a tumbleweed

I am a tumbleweed storyteller
born in the North.
I learnt there to walk.
Many places saw me
sauntering along,
many people
gave me their stories.

One day I met Condor
who yarned about the South,
places of mystery,
magic and unbeknown.

"Can you tell me
how I can get there?"
I asked.
"No, when you are ready,
you will know."
He said.

I kept on dreaming

of the world of magic,

I kept on wandering

with a yearning in my heart,

but I could not find directions,

I could not find the South.

One day I got weary

of my quest,

I let the wind carry me away

and I fell asleep.

And when I opened my eyes

I was there…

The garden

The ancient garden was once full of beauties.
A gardener treated it tenderly every day
and it was the most beautiful and
perfect garden on Earth.

One day the gardener got sick.
He tended the plants less and
forgot the trees.
The beauty of the garden silently started to wear.

One day the gardener died.
The garden got covered by vine and weed
and nobody recognized
it was a garden before.

One day the owner of the garden woke up.
He felt something was missing.
He walked to the place
where once the garden stood
and started to weed.

With every move

he found something thought to be lost,

with every move

beauty was revealed.

The garden slowly came back to life

and now he is the gardener of his own heart.

The door of now

You are standing in the door of now.

It is open.

You decide to step forward

into your mystery

or to step back, close the door

and continue living in illusion.

The masquerade

A pile of trash left in the desert
tells the sad story of a fugitive family.

Unspoken words tell more
than a book of novels.

A piece of wood hides a powerful spirit.
In an old man appear a warrior and a child.

Life around is a masquerade.
We do not know with whom we dance
until we look beneath the masks.

Most of us dance our entire life
in the world of disguise
without knowing
who our partners are.

Our eyes are shut

to magic and dreams,

our eyes are blind

to the essence of life.

We see only

when we look

beyond the visible.

We see only

when we choose

to see.

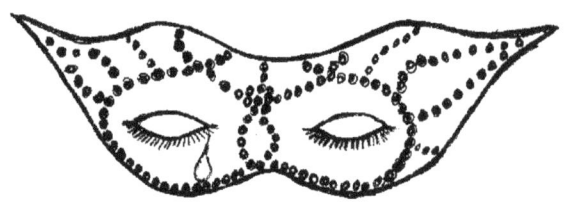

Running into the deep forest

I am like the deer
that is running into the deep forest.
The branches of thoughts
scratch my skin, make me bleed
and slow down my gallop.

I stop at the deepest clearing
and look at myself
bleeding from scratches of a lifetime.
Some wounds are fresh
and some have become deep scars.

But it was I,
who stepped into the traps on my way.
It was I,
who directed my gallop
against those trees.

It was I,

who decided to follow my mind

against my heart;

and it was I,

who feared more than I realized.

As I see myself

in the mirror of my own eyes

I can continue running

as I did in my entire life.

But the silence will haunt me,

the silence of knowing:

I am responsible

for all the pain in my life...

Shadow and light

Shadow and light
Shadow and light
They live side by side
in the sun and the clouds,
in the day and the night,
in my mind and my heart.

Shadow and light
Shadow and light
Play together, in a constant dance
with the air and the time.
One feeds the other,
one dies in the other.

Shadow and light
Shadow and light
Don't exist without the other.
They are one
in the illusion of separation.
I wonder they know.

Shadow and light
Shadow and light
As I make my life's mistakes,
as I go through love and hate
I can see them playing
in my mind and my heart.

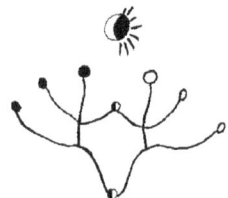

Shadow and light
Shadow and light
I wonder they realize
that I can alter their dance
by changing
the source of my light.

I can elevate my light
to decrease shadow.
I can increase intensity
of the light I spread, and
I can change my focus
from shadow to light.

The story of a tree

The little seeds of the tree

are waiting…

and waiting…

and waiting…

for the raindrops to fall
to bring them to life.

As the rain begins to fall
there begins a new life.
First in the seed
the tree begins to dance.

As the shell gets too small
the tree bursts out to feel more.
It grows roots, trunk, branches and leaves.
It feels the earth,
it feels the sun.

As time goes by, the tree grows.

It dances alone.

The young tree enjoys its dance.

It bends far, makes big moves.

Its branches are flexible and fast,

all winds they can withstand.

Its music is the wind

and its rhythm are the sun and the stars.

And the tree just dances, day and night.

As time goes by, the tree grows up.

Its bark gets thicker; its branches are now tall.

It learns subtle moves and

feels the dance.

Its dance is now more soft,

gentle, considerate and wise.

The tree dances with other trees,

it dances with the birds,

it dances with the wind.

It also enjoys watching

its own branches and leaves dance.

The tree is now mature
birds are nesting on its branch.

Its music is the wind
and its rhythm are the sun and the stars.
And the tree just dances, day and night.

As time goes by, the tree grows old.
Even a subtle move now hurts.
The bark is just getting too hard.
Even a gentle breeze of wind brings pain
but the tree still wants to dance.
Its music is the wind
and its rhythm are the sun and the stars.
It now enjoys more
watching other trees dance
or just watches its own leaves
playing in the wind.

It knows the day is close
when even a small touch of wind
will be the end

But it still does not forget to dance,
even in pain the old tree dances
with the wind, the sun and the stars.

One day that last touch of wind comes
and the tree falls.
Nothing is left behind, just an empty tree trunk.
The spirit of the tree is now flying high.

But as the tree fell
it spread its seeds with the wind.

They fell on the ground.

And they are waiting…
and waiting…
and waiting…

for the raindrops to fall
to bring them to life.

As the rain begins to fall

there begins a new life.

First in the seed

the tree begins to dance.

This is the story of a tree, and

this is the circle of life.

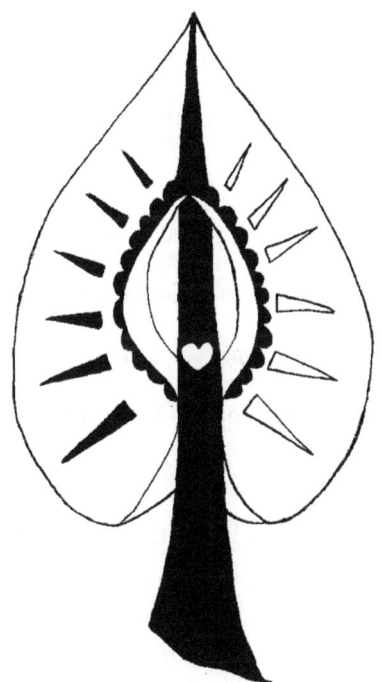

Subtleties

A look can make a caterpillar

leave its climb for knowledge.

A touch can express

the entire world of a man.

A smell from a long unopened bottle

can bring a lost Dad back to life.

Singing the anthem

can pull a nation together,

and I can never forget the taste of the first kiss.

When I look back to the memories of my life

what I remember most

is not what was learnt or said.

What I remember are the subtle moments.

The subtleties colored the outline of my life,

and it is my choice

to live life in rainbow

or black and white.

Even then, I still spent
too much time in my brain
not realizing my thoughts
withheld many new moments to be born.

There are no more moments to waste.

The lessons of love and life
need to be experienced, and
not lived by control
and by my head.

Flow

Born innocent into this world
like fresh spring water
with your song of loud gurgles you start to run
towards the ocean of your dreams.

Grown first to stream, then to river
joined by many other streams
you are adrift in the bed laid down before you
and you drift everything in your way.

As you grow bigger and older
your flow slows down by your silted bed,
your song becomes a silent memory
and the ocean an unattainable dream.

Leave your bed to conquer fresh lands
before the silt makes you still.
Let the world hear the song of your flow
and your ocean will welcome you one day.

Silence

Silence is power
when it is there
or when it is missing.

Silence is full of songs
inside and outside,
can you hear them?

Silence is a powerful
teacher,
difficult to find.

But when you meet,
it gives you
your world.

Tomorrow

If tomorrow I had to die
would I really care
who should have taken the trash out
or whose fault it was?
Or would I just love today?

If tomorrow I had to die
would I really care
about my life purpose
and the philosophies of life?
Or would I just fully experience life today?

If tomorrow I had to die
would I continue delaying
love, dreams, truth
that I put off as life went by?
Or would I just realize them today?

I take tomorrow for granted

believing there is time.

But that last today could be this day,

do I live it that way?

Reflection

Words are

reflections

of one's mind.

Do you see

the truth

behind the reflection?

Or do you reflect on

the reflection,

the mere words?

STORIES

OF

LOVE

Something ended

I am deeply hurt.
I did not even notice
my soul and my feelings
were not understood for a long time,
nor received respect
from the one I loved.
I shared all I was
with all my confidence and trust,
and this instant I realize
how wrong I was
and I break down in tears.

But I can't deny who I am
whatever they say,
I know my love was genuine
and they betrayed.
I know I have to move on
I can't deny my light,
and through my pain
I decide to clean
the garden of my heart.

The weeds of past

root deep inside of me.

If I pull them fast

the roots will break

and stay behind

as the soil of my garden is hard.

A good gardener waters the soil first.

The water softens the soil

and helps him to remove those roots.

Without water

the weeds will never pass.

I know now

how wrong I was all the time

trying to overcome my hurt alone.

Only heart can heal the heart

but the healer heart is not my own....

A tale of love

There was a tree once.
A young, beautiful tree
that stood in the forest of love
along the path of life.

She loved when the travelers
stopped on their way
to sit in her shade
sometimes alone, sometimes with a mate.

She was listening to their stories,
the stories of their hearts.
She loved and cried with them.
She felt their lives.

The travelers sat for a while,
their hearts were filled with love;
then they left, changed,
to continue their path.

Alone, on a search
one day a young girl came,
then an old man sat down
tired of lifelong pain.

They turned to each other,
they started to talk.
He taught her his wisdom,
she reminded him to love.

Although they were different
the tree felt their hearts,
their outlook was just a disguise,
both of them were young and wise.

The tree decided to make magic
to pull together those hearts.
It happened right in front of their eyes,
they slowly came to realize.

The tree smiled and asked the stars
to shed more light in their nights

as they both were still asleep
in the illusion of their lives.

They were both dreaming:
their hearts were bleeding through their past,
their future from fears was paralyzed.
"Wake up" – the tree gently asked.

The girl woke up and looked at him.
She saw him struggle in his dream.
She nudged him and nudged him
to wake him up from his sleep.

He noticed her nudging, grumpily.
He opened his eyes for a while
but the dream was stronger than his new love,
his eyes were closed for the light.

One day she got weary of nudging.
She was seen angry, not who she was.
She looked at him with sorrow
and asked the tree what to do.

The tree answered:
"Stop nudging, my dear.
He knows he is in a dream, and
he has his free will to wake or stay."

The words of the tree broke her heart,
but she knew the tree was right.
She stood up and looked at him
sadly, hoping she could walk with him.

She thanked the tree for the magic,
she thanked the moments of love.
Grieving a new dream of a joint journey
she set off, alone, on the path of life.

She has gone far, to far-away lands
but she could not forget about him.
He was still in her mind and her heart.
Her mind wondered:

Will he ever wake up?
Would he then want to find her?

How will he look like then?
Will she want to be with him then?

The answers to her questions
are mystery, until future becomes now.
Even now is mystery
as she left him dreaming under the tree.

Today holds the seeds of the answers
to the questions of all mystery.
Say, do, think and feel now
what you want your answers to be.

Love is not a mystery
when felt deeply through the heart,
it is your reality, part of who you are,
not felt for a return or a reward.

Goodbye

The moment I say goodbye
wishing the best from my heart
a little piece in me dies.

I know the source I give from
is infinite and they love
but saying goodbye
still takes that little piece of my heart.

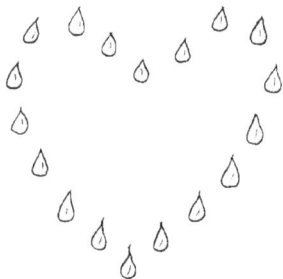

Every little piece counts,
every little piece is a teardrop in my eyes.

To Kendall and Tomek

The bird of freedom

The little bird was walking in the yard
afraid, with a broken wing.
He saw me coming, trying to help him.
He knew my capture would lead him to fly
but he was afraid, and moved away.

It took a while until I got close
and finally I picked him up,
but not knowing any better, I put him into a cage.
The little bird first went along
but soon he got restless and
flew against the safety of the cage.

I took him out and set him free.
I surrendered him to his destiny.
He didn't know what to do with that freedom.
He tried his wings and walked a little
then moved into the invisible cage of a bush
and stood still.

The next day I found his feathers
covering my lawn, everywhere.
I mourned my little bird
and all moments we shared together.
I asked what his last wish from me was
and I heard he wanted to see me dance.

I danced crying, I fell on the ground,
I danced shaking from tears in my heart.
I danced for him, beyond myself,
I wanted to give him that last wish he deserved.
And I felt him watching me.

I danced for long till the tears started to fade
and my heart started to feel
the beauty of us and the world around.
I saw my little bird with the eyes of joy
and not just through my sorrow.

And in that moment
he walked out of the bush, alive.

I could not believe my eyes.
And again, I started to cry.

The bird headed to the light, no more shadow.
He freely moved, picking food he found.
He was free, even with his broken wing.
He defied death
and taught a lesson to me.

Through my tears I saw myself
how my heart was broken, like his little wing, and
how many times I went for that invisible cage.
I can be free, even with a broken heart.

But the old must first die,
and I should not be afraid of moving to the light...

When eyes meet

When eyes meet
there is a spark
that can lead anywhere
to friendship, to war, to love.
I never know…

When eyes meet
that spark can change a life
that spark can ignite body and heart
and can light the fire of love.
In its light even my shadow looks beautiful,
and I dance smiling, naked under the moon.

When eyes meet a journey begins
on a path we don't know where it leads.
We never know how far we walk together
and what we will see,
just hold my hand and walk with me…

Inspired by Joanne Shenandoah's song with the same title

The gift

The gift is in front of me
wrapped, I can't see inside.
I look at the wrapping.
It looks soft and attractive, but
some parts are crinkled and rough.
The gift calls, "I am yours", but
I just sit and don't WANT to open it.

The gift is still in front of me
wrapped, I can't see inside.
I get curious, and scrape the surface a little.
I look inside.
As the hole is too small
I can only see a silhouette,
shadow still overwhelms it all.
The gift calls, "I am yours", but
I just sit, now AFRAID to open it.

I look at the silhouette in my gift.
It brings up feelings of love and joy,

but it also puts me to a place
of confusion and sorrow.
The gift still calls, "I am yours", but
I just sit, STILL AFRAID to open it.

I want to see more, and
I increase the hole on the box.
I put my hand into the hole and
I touch the silhouette.
The first moment it feels soft, like velvet, but
as I go beneath I have to pull my hand out
as it is bleeding from a sting.
The gift still calls, "I am yours", but
I just sit, now CONFUSED AND HURT to open it.

I want to know now what's inside,
I tear the wrapping and
I OPEN the box.

I look at my ROSE now, in the light.

Can I accept it has thorns, with the beauty it got,
or will I put it back into the box?

No words

There are no words

to express the deepest feelings,

the wonders I see

to make you understand

how it feels to see the first Christmas tree,

how I feel when the warm rain touches my skin,

how I feel when I dance with a dragonfly,

how I feel when I am held by the man I love.

Words cannot describe

the essence of feelings and mystery.

They just draw an empty outline

or destroy it

when spoken not from the heart.

Come closer,

look into my eyes,

see me smile and see me cry,

hear my heartbeat, hear me sing,

listen to what's behind my words,
feel my touch and feel my skin,
watch me walk my life.

See and feel me
and you will understand.

Because of you

I am thinking of you in the morning,
I am thinking of you in the night.
You are on my mind while I am awake,
You are on my mind when I dream.
You are with me everywhere I go,
You hold my hand in everything I do.
I might be far away from you
but you are with me, in me,
because I am who I am now
because of you.

A late smile

Like the raindrops under the tree
that are now dry, but left a mark in the sand
my tears of sadness reached a gentle heart
and there a deep wound they stung.

The gentle heart just gave and gave,
newborn flowers, hope and the rivers of life.
Love itself appeared as him,
he wanted to see me again smile.

But blinded by my own sorrow
my heart was shut
and like the smoke of a dying fire
I brought uncried tears into his eyes.

Now being alone I feel what it meant
his touch, his words and what is left unspoken.
I cry now for two bleeding hearts, and
his hurts me more than mine.

I wish I could turn back time

to hold his hands and look deeply in his eyes.

After his first heartfelt words

I would tell him how much he meant

and would give him a smile from my heart.

The miracle of love

Love is like

raindrops to the desert.

When it rains,

it transforms the entire landscape

and brings out its most incredible beauty.

Heart

Heart.... what a sensitive place,
the source of love and hate,
the source of give and take.
Which way to go?
Who decides? Heart, mind or pride?

What makes a warrior of the heart?
What distinguishes him from a refugee, a coward?
Where is the fine line between the two?
When decisions made through the heart,
when heart-decisions break hearts?

What conducts the heart's actions?
What directs love?
When we live and act
we follow our hearts,
but what or who does our heart follow?
Do we know?

Waves of the ocean

I am like the ocean
with waves of feelings
in constant motion.
I climb high, then into my depth I fall.
Even in the moments of stillness
my feelings are cradled, sleepless.

My feelings are vast and strong
like the waves of the ocean.
They embrace life, the travelers
but when stirred by a storm
my power is given to the elements
and I destroy all.

I love and live
like the waves of the ocean
in constant motion
with ups and downs,

with embrace and destruction,

with bliss and frustration.

I am born of water

like the waves of the ocean

fluid, in constant motion.

Could I exist with no waves at all?

When I love with waves

do I really love at all?

You and I

Like the Sun that strokes the horizon
and the fields in the morning,
first gently, then with an intensified light,
You came to my life.

I was like the pond
with cool waters and gifts of fresh lotus flowers,
I felt the touch of your morning rays.

First I danced along with my surface.
As time passed by, your light heated my waters,
stirred up those cool currents
and transformed my waves.

I was a mirror to your light
and through your reflection I also saw myself,
I was holding onto the water-drops that left me
not knowing what to do with that intense light
that lit up my days and my heart.

During the night, when only stars light the sky

    my currents are still.

    I am dreaming of the Sun

    and those stirred up waves.

    I see what was below the surface

        beneath that stirring,

        and when I awake

    I look right into your eyes.

Tell me everything

"Tell me everything."
You ask me.
I have so much to tell,
do not even know where to start,
to tell you about my journeys, my dreams,
my feelings, my life
to ask you about your journeys, your dreams,
your feelings, your life.

"Tell me everything."
You ask me with a smile
and a spark in your eyes.
As I look into those eyes
I am immersed in your look
and I just sit, holding your hand
and forget everything,
every thought I wanted to say or ask.
They matter no more.

"Tell me everything."

You ask me and

I tell nothing.

I just feel you and the moment

wanting to be there,

wanting to be with you.

Forever.

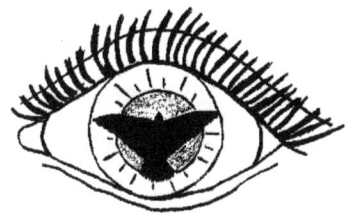

Mirrors

I can see you

when I see myself clearly,

when I understand my reflection in your mirror,

when I open the blinds on my eyes.

I can see you

when I see myself clearly.

Be my mirror; help me see myself like the hawk

and I will make you fly.

Long distance relationship

There is a distance of space between us.
The street that parted us when we first met
now has become the Atlantic Ocean,
but the distance feels the same.

The street already felt like an ocean once
as we were stranded on its opposite shores.
I looked forward to your crossing every morning,
I looked forward to your embrace with anticipation
and every step felt like forever.

Now we need to fly to see each other
or I can see and hear you on my screen
tricked by the illusion of my eyes that you are close,
but when I touch you, my fingers hit a lifeless machine
instead of the warmth of your skin.

But I choose to dream while I am awake,
I choose the illusion without the blood,
as I know that all is real,
there is no distance
between our hearts.

Missing you

I wish I could contain the smell of the honeysuckle
as its fragrance glows at dusk in my garden.
I wish I could contain the colors of the sunset
as they reflect the clouds above my home.
I wish I could contain the songs of the birds and the crickets
as shadow starts to cover the skies.
I wish I could contain the light of the first stars
as darkness falls into the night.
I wish I could gift you all these moments
so that you can share them, with me.

I wish you could sit here, beside me.
Close, that I could feel you
through your breath and your heartbeat
through your touch, your words and your silence
through your presence and your distant journey
through the light and the shadow in your eyes
through your love towards me.
God, I miss you deeply...

Our journey

I have been walking with him for a while,
some months, but maybe some lifetime.
We share a journey, our thoughts and feelings,
but I still don't know him.

Every moment his newness unfolds
and I see him growing.
I look into his eyes
and wonder what he sees.

I am a fresh flower
with many buds still to blossom.
Does he like what he sees now
or what this flower can become?

Does he love the now,
or does he love the dream,
the dream of the unborn flowers
he hasn't even seen?

We can dream of love,

but should not expect,

the newborn flower is beautiful

when born in blue, and not red.

When love exists, colors do not matter

just the blossom we bring out from one another,

to make their beauty complete with our touch,

to make their journey unforgettable with us.

ABOUT THE AUTHOR

Andrea Balint was born and studied in Budapest, Hungary. She is a finance professional who spent over eight years working, teaching and traveling in Europe, America, Africa and Asia.

In 2004 a sickness changed the focus of her life. She turned from a career focus to spirituality to find balance and harmony and to realize her childhood dreams that were about making the world a better place via creativity and teaching. She participated in volunteer teaching in India; she has become a practitioner and teacher of Reiki, Seichem and Angel energy healing as well as opened a webshop that sells her crafts and an author. She first wrote children's stories, and inspired by Lench Archuleta she started to write and illustrate poems during her first visit to Arizona in May, 2010.

You can contact the author at andrea.balint@live.com.

THANK YOU!

www.ingramcontent.com/pod-product-compliance
Lightning Source LLC
Chambersburg PA
CBHW031358160426
42813CB00090B/3140/J